Alicia — My
Search For Peace

Alicia — My Search For Peace

Alicia Simpson

Christian Focus Publications Ltd.

Published by
Christian Focus Publications Ltd

Tain   **Houston**
Ross-shire   **Texas**

© **1989 Christian Focus Publications Ltd.**

ISBN 0906 731 86 0

ACKNOWLEDGMENTS

The publishers would like to express special thanks to Mrs Janice Davison, Perth for her assistance in the preparation of this project for publication.

CONTENTS

PREFACE

To many an upbringing in a convent between the wars, and the personal search for inner peace within the confines of the Roman Catholic Church, may appear very foreign. Alicia Simpson's story is, however, found in that setting. It tells of one woman's search for peace, denied her in childhood and eluding her in adult life. It is an account of tragedy, frustration and human failure, set in the confines of a religious life.

The great value of Alicia's life is the light she sheds, not on a particular religious framework but rather on the assurance that God's transforming power may be experienced by any, however unworthy. It records the gratitude of one who knew a genuine life-changing encounter with Jesus Christ — a Jesus she had known of from infancy, yet did not know personally until her life all but fell apart.

Though few will relate exactly to the individual details of her story, I trust that Alicia's search for peace will speak to many whose lives are equally in need of her Saviour. As you will see, this does not just include the irreligious, but all too often the most religious of all. It was so in Christ's days upon earth and remains so today.

Alicia is now with the Lord who found her. This, her story, has been taken from a talk she gave before she died, in which she desired to be faithful in recording what God had done for her soul. May the Lord's love and faithfulness here recorded lead others to trust Him.

Phil Roberts.

Chapter 1

Go And Tell

'Let the redeemed of the Lord say so.' Psalm 107 v.2.
How often are the redeemed reluctant to say so!

Perhaps no-one could have been more reluctant at
one time to say so than myself. I just couldn't believe
that I should ever have to make this story known. I
couldn't believe that a past, which I thought was dead,
buried and forgotten, would have to be revealed. It
was the last thing on this earth that I wanted to do; but
arguing with the Lord is a futile occupation, for, even
if you are a woman, you do not get the last word! So,
as one whom He had redeemed from the hand of the
enemy, there came for me the day when I had to say so
publicly. Even as a trembling woman of old once had
to admit in front of a vast crowd who were thronging
to the Lord Jesus that she had been made whole, there
came to me the command to go and tell: 'Go and tell
what great things the Lord hath done for thee'.

In Chapter 9 of John's Gospel we have what is, to
my mind, the most outstanding picture in the whole of
the New Testament of the born again believer — the
beggar whose eyes the Lord Jesus opened on the
Sabbath day. Our Lord Himself tells us why He
worked this miracle on that particular man: it was that
the works of God should be shown in him.

Ought not this to be true of every person on whom
the Lord Jesus, by his Holy Spirit, has worked the
miracle of new birth, opening their eyes to the

Saviour? Surely in each one of us too the works of God should be seen, and that is the only reason which encourages me to tell this story — not that you should know all about what I did, but that you should marvel at the works of God. This is a testimony to the saving power of the God who deals with the hopeless situation.

The seventh verse of Psalm 107 tells us that; 'He led them forth by the right way that they might go to a city of habitation'.

This verse is always the theme of my testimony.

Chapter 2

Childhood Memories

In order that you may understand the background from which I came and all that followed, it is necessary to start with a brief mention of my childhood, which was far from pleasant.

I was born into a Roman Catholic household. As a child I knew nothing but abuse and ill-treatment from a mother, a father and then a step-father, of whom I was terrified. Because they were people well-known in business and musical circles, their cruelty was never discovered.

When the time came for schooling I was sent to a convent. It was run by nuns whose lives were dedicated to the Blessed Virgin Mary. The emphasis of the religious education was on devotion to Our Lady. All the special feast days of Our Lady (and there are many of them in the course of a year) were celebrated with much pomp and ceremonial with her statues being dressed up with lace, jewels, flowers and lighted candles. The highest honour one could attain in that school was to be one of those to strew rose petals before the statue of Our Lady, as it was carried in procession around the convent grounds.

Great stress was laid on the fact that, after confession of one's sins to a priest, salvation depended almost entirely upon the intercession of the Mother of God. We addressed her in our hymns and prayers as the Refuge of Sinners, the Queen of Heaven, the Star of the Sea, the Mother of Mercy, our Advocate, our Life, our Sweetness, our Hope, and by countless other titles. Oh yes, we could tell you that the Lord Jesus died and shed His blood for the remission of sins, and that He is God, the second person of the Blessed Trinity; but we were taught that only the Blessed Virgin Mary could make that blood available for us. Although this is not official Roman Catholic teaching, many Catholics believe that Mary co-operated in the work of redemption and so is said to be co-redemptrix with her Son; that to her has been committed the ministry of reconciliation; and that she stands between us and an angry God the Father, aided by the saints who can help to plead our cause.

Knowing nothing whatever of the love of parents, of a happy home, or happy school days — for most of the nuns in the school I attended were anything but kind — weekdays were spent in misery at the convent and weekends were spent in hell at home. You can imagine what kind of ideas I had about God. We gabbled off endless repetitions of 'Our Father which art in heaven'. If He up there was anything like the two fathers I knew down here, then heaven was a place to which I had no desire to go.

If introduction to Roman Catholicism began in earnest for me when I started school, then at the age of eighteen I was to be plunged into it up to the neck. By the time I had reached that age, life had dealt me every possible blow and I wanted no more of it. So I made a desperate attempt at suicide.

My last conscious thought was that I would be going straight to hell. The next thing I knew was that I hadn't gone to hell; I was still here, and in a hospital bed.

That wasn't going to be the way that my life would end.

Psalm 107 says: 'He brought them out of darkness and the shadow of death'.

At the time, however, I knew nothing but the bitterest disappointment that I had not ended it all and that I was back in a world where I didn't want to be. In those days I was under age, and the authorities soon traced my mother; but she wasn't interested, couldn't have cared less, and did not want me back. They had enquired, of course, what religion I was. Naturally, I told them I was a Roman Catholic, so I was placed in the charge of a Roman Catholic probation officer as being in need of care and protection.

When I had recovered sufficiently, I left. The probation officer, I suppose, did not know what to do with me. I was now without home, friends, or money. Probably wanting to get me off her hands as soon as possible, she asked me if I would go to a convent for a few weeks in order to have a period of convalescence to get properly back on my feet again. She would come and talk over what I was to do in the future. I couldn't have cared less at the time what I was to do in the future, and for the present I didn't care where I went either, so I consented to go to the convent, which she assured me would be ideal for recovery.

Chapter 3

Convent Days

The day duly arrived when the probation officer called for me and took me to the convent. Behind me the doors shut. I was eighteen, and I was not to see the outside world again until I was thirty-six years of age. What she had taken me to was a Roman Catholic penitentiary! A more ghastly place it would be difficult to describe. Inside this 'religious institution', such things as Christian love, mercy, kindness and concern for one another were unknown and never experienced. It was a place of hard work, the most hideous uniform, unspeakable living conditions and severe punishment for the slightest infringement of any of the rules. Not only were my own clothes taken away from me, but I was even stripped of my own name and was called by a Roman Catholic saint's name instead. Thus was my identity lost.

Shut away in there we were forced to do heavy manual work, which brought in a considerable revenue to the convent. We also had to do a great deal of penance, as it is called, in order to try to earn forgiveness for our sins. We had to rise early and go to Mass in the convent chapel, not only on Sundays, but on every single day of the week. We had to work all day in strict silence, and woe betide any of us caught talking or passing written notes to one another! Our scanty meals were eaten in silence while someone read aloud from the lives of the saints.

On a few special feast days we were allowed a little extra food as a treat, the light-fingered ones being watched to see they didn't steal some of what was on a neighbour's plate. Only on Sundays were we allowed to read anything for ourselves, unless we had been deprived of the privilege as a punishment for some misdemeanour. Our reading matter was exclusively Roman Catholic books. In all the years I was shut away I never saw a newspaper. Nobody representing either Government or council ever set foot in the place, so no-one knew what was going on inside it.

When I realised how I had been tricked, I suddenly came to life again. Life became sweet, and I now wanted to hang on to it and to get out. I did put up a desperate struggle to get out, but it was useless, and only made matters worse for me. If I did get out where was I to go? The nuns knew well that I was without a friend in the world and that no one would ever come and claim me. In the end I resigned myself to being there for the rest of my life.

I turned to the only consolation that was left me — religion. This consisted for the most part of praying to statues and pictures of the Blessed Virgin Mary and the saints — I believed that all this devotion to the statues of Our Lady and the saints was the right way to go about getting peace with God. As a Roman Catholic I was striving after something that eluded me.

Chapter 4

The Search For Peace

In the convent I was eventually made a Child of Mary as a reward for good conduct. I knew nothing, however, of being made a child of God. Roman Catholic practices such as attending Mass, going to confession, adoration of the Blessed Virgin Mary and the saints, did not bring me closer to God. Sin remained as an insurmountable barrier between us. In spite of accepting the hardships of my life as a penance for what I'd done, try as I would, I could not get peace with God nor feel any forgiveness for my sins. No matter what I did, that barrier remained between me and that dread Being up there of whom I was so afraid.

The years went by and time became meaningless. I don't remember now what age I was when the idea first entered my head that I wanted to become a nun, but gradually I became aware that it was there, and it stayed there. Surely if I could become a nun and live a life of complete dedication to God I could earn forgiveness for my sins and find the right way to peace with Him? Little did I dream then that one day I would discover how to become 'right with God'; and it would have nothing to do with convents, or nuns, or life in a religious order.

How was I to become a nun? I had no money, and girls and women who wished to enter Roman Catholic religious orders usually had to take a considerable sum of money in with them as a dowry, since they were becoming 'brides of Christ.' But I hadn't a penny. I had no position in life, no friends or relations to pull strings on my behalf, and I was in a most unrespectable place for anyone wanting to be a nun. I was amongst the very dregs of Roman Catholic girls and women. But this 'bee I had got into my bonnet' persisted. Somehow I was determined that, however much circumstances were against me, I was going to find a way of becoming a nun.

In the end I was allowed to make my request known to Mother Superior. To my great joy at the time, she told me that there was just one religious order open to someone like me — a strictly enclosed Third Order of Carmelites, a very penitential order. Since I was not going to get out into the world again, I would be allowed to enter it.

In due course I was transferred, simply removed from A to B in a closed car. Eventually I became known as Sister Magdalene of the Passion. I entered full of enthusiasm and great ideas, but it didn't take me long to lose the lot, for I did not find in there the kind of life I had expected. Nor did I find what I had gone to seek — peace with God.

If I didn't find peace in the convent I did find plenty of penance. Three times a week we thrashed ourselves with knotted whips — a constitutional rule of the order. We had to kneel to the Mistress of Novices or the Mother Superior, to kiss the floor before we were allowed to eat. Sometimes we ate our dinner off the floor. These and many other extraordinary actions were supposed to make atonement for our sins, bring us into favour with Our Lady and the saints and earn a higher place in heaven. So, our whole lives were devoted to doing penances for our sins, and to devotions centred mainly round the worship of Mary. Since there was no infallible Word of God to believe in but only the pronouncements of an 'infallible' Pope, our faith was pinned on all sorts of religious objects, the Scriptures being replaced by the most fantastic stories of the lives of the saints.

When I look back now to the absurdities and impossiblilities of these stories which I accepted without question, I am appalled. The Russians claim that Gagarin was the first man into space. Did you know that a man was up there, without a space suit, hundreds of years before Gagarin? A monk called Dominic went up into space in the Middle Ages and landed on a cloud. Our Lady came and met him there and handed him a rosary, (a string of five sets of ten beads with a crucifix on the end). Our lady told Dominic to take the rosary back to earth, gave him instructions about what prayers were to be said on it and promised all sorts of wonderful favours to those who practised devotion to it. One of the treasured holy pictures given to me on my twenty-first birthday in the penitentiary was a pictorial representation of this amazing event.

We believed that the saints had all kinds of magical powers. There was once a certain saint who taught a bird to say 'Hail Mary'. One day when the bird was out flying a hawk swooped down on it. The terrified bird screamed out 'Hail Mary' and the hawk dropped dead. Now the teaching behind this is, if the Mother of God will save a bird who can say 'Hail Mary', how much more will she be ready and willing to save any person who calls upon her name?

Seven times a day, in the convent chapel, we chanted in Latin the Office of the Blessed Virgin

Mary, as it was called. This was done in the bodily presence of the Lord Jesus, whom we firmly believed was upon the altar in the form of communion bread, as He is supposed to be on every Roman Catholic altar throughout the world. We worshipped this bread, spending hours in devotion before it, often prostrate on our faces.

We sang our hymns in Latin to the divine being on the altar called 'Blessed Sacrament' and practised all sorts of penances and devotions before it. We also practised various devotions and prayers to our favourite saints, praying with great fervour that Britain would return to the worship of the Mother of God and become known once more as the 'dowry of Mary' as it had been called in the Middle Ages.

Chapter 5

First Steps to Freedom

Steadily I began to sicken of a kind of life that was getting me nowhere. There seemed to be so much 'performance' of religion and so little of anything that was real. Deep down inside me was the desire for something deeper, a longing for something that was eluding me. I couldn't name it, or put a finger on it. I didn't know what it was, but something was causing me the greatest uneasiness and dissatisfaction. Instinctively I seemed to know that, whatever it was that I wanted, I wasn't going to get it in that convent, so I determined that, come what may I was going to get back into the world again. How I was going to do this I had no idea at the time, but an inner conviction was telling me that I was in the wrong place.

Over thirty years ago it was considered a great scandal for an enclosed nun to throw up the religious life and return to the world after being clothed with the habit of an order and pronounced 'the bride of Christ'. There are, of course, orders of nuns who go in for school teaching, hospital work, running orphanages and such like. These nuns naturally go about the world and have contact with people, but in a Contemplative Order, such as I was in, there is no communication with the outside world at all. One is supposed to have left it for ever. If I had wanted to leave I should have done so whilst still a postulant, during the first six months of entering. But then I would have just been sent back to the penitentiary, and I didn't exactly relish that idea. There was one thing, however, I had not done: I had not taken final vows, and nothing would induce me to do so.

Obedience to superiors is the rule of life in these places, and to dare to go against their decisions and to think for oneself is a mortal sin and not to be tolerated. The vow of obedience taken by men and women in Roman Catholic religious orders is a vow taken to obey, not God, but one's religious superiors. I began to question this, and I began to question many other things also. I began to discover that I had a mind of my own, and that mind was absolutely made up that I was going to get out. Being in a Protestant country and not having taken my final vows, I could not be kept in against my will, but I had much to go through before I was released. Nowadays, I know, nothing is thought of a nun leaving her convent. The winds of change have blown over the surface of the Roman Catholic Church, but in the days I'm speaking of, had I taken final vows, I would have been excommunicated on the spot.

It's best to pass over all I went through before I came out of that convent, but in the end out I came, thirty-six years of age, into a world of war and into the heart of London, which was getting the worst of it. Thus was the first step taken on the long, long journey towards finding the right way to obtain peace with God. But, it must be noted that I had not seen the light when I came out of that convent, and many years were to elapse before I did so.

I was in disgrace with Holy Mother Church, and absolutely sickened with religion, which had failed me. Almost immediately my age group had to register for war work and, not wishing to go into the armed services, I was sent to aeroplane engineering. I was bitter, disillusioned, friendless, homeless and penniless. I had almost forgotten my own name. I was under the continual strain of the war, and often I said to myself, 'The next bomb that drops is going to have my name on it, and who cares anyway?' Nevertheless, though I could hardly have cared less at the time as the buildings crashed around me, again and again my life was preserved and brought out of the shadow of death: for to be killed in an air-raid, without the knowledge of salvation, was not in God's plan for me.

Chapter 6

An Unhappy Marriage

I had tried to serve God as I thought right, by living a
religious life and entering a religious order. I had tried
desperately to earn my way to heaven and I had failed
miserably. Religious life seemed a mockery; there was
nothing in it. All my devotion to Our Lady and the
saints had come to nothing so, in disgust, I turned
against religion. I stopped going to Mass on Sundays,
flung up all practice of religion, and became what is
known as a lapsed Roman Catholic.

Soon I was transferred to Scotland on war work,
and there I eventually met a man, a widower, who
asked me to marry him. For the first time in my life I
was being offered a chance of security, a home of my
own, a name, an opportunity to settle down and take
root somewhere — all the things in life that had passed
me by! The offer was too good to refuse. I might never
get another one, so I grasped it as a drowning man
clutches at a straw. I accepted only for the sake of
getting those things I had never had. This man was a
Protestant, very 'religious', an elder of his church, but
a man who like myself knew nothing whatever of
salvation. Immediately after my acceptance of his
proposal, we married. Perhaps, you may think, that
might have been the end of all my troubles and things
would soon have worked out all right for me. Instead,
it was out of the frying pan and into the fire.

Our marriage was disastrous from the word go. It

wasn't long before I experienced the truth of the saying 'marry in haste and repent at leisure'. When, for the first time in my life, I stood in a Protestant church to be married, my knees were knocking and my husband had no idea that he was marrying a Roman Catholic and an ex-nun. Had he known, I'm perfectly certain that he would have committed murder on the spot, as he was a Freemason. As for me, I half expected the roof to fall in during the ceremony because I was marrying a Protestant! A Roman Catholic who marries a Protestant has to get a special dispensation to do so, and even then the marriage must be conducted by a Roman Catholic priest or the couple are not regarded as being married at all. I was committing mortal sin, and, if I died suddenly before I could get to confession to tell the priest, I would go straight to hell. Hence my relief when I got outside that church and the roof hadn't fallen in on top of me! Although I had lapsed and wasn't going to Mass, I still believed that the Roman Catholic church was the only true church, outside of which there was no salvation, and that everybody who wasn't a Roman Catholic was a heretic.

One of the things I soon discovered about the heretic I had married was that among his pet hates was Roman Catholics. The very name was an abomination in his ears, and aroused him to fury, so I didn't ever dare to tell him he had married one.

At that time, only a very narrow road separated our house from the Forth and Clyde canal, and anything that annoyed my husband, who was a man of very fiery temper, was flung with scant ceremony out of the window and into the canal — and he had a very good aim! It was no wonder that I didn't dare to tell him I was a Roman Catholic — that canal was far too handy! Nevertheless, after that initial visit to a Protestant church to get married, I wouldn't go again. I didn't want to pile up mortal sins, or there would be far too many to tell the priest when I got to confession again. The thought was buried at the back of my mind: some day I knew it would have to be either confession or hell for all eternity. But I couldn't get to confession just then; it would have to wait till a more convenient time and place.

Things went from bad to worse, and I bitterly regretted the step I had taken in such haste. Would nothing ever come right for me? Unhappiness drove me once more to think about God and eternity and what awaited me on the other side of the grave. Like the prophet Jonah, when my soul fainted within me, I remembered the Lord.

I began to think that the misery of my married life was a punishment from God for what I had done by marrying outside the church of Rome. The more I thought about it, the more I longed once again to try to get right with God.

I had heard in my younger days so many sermons preached on hell that, to me, it was a very terrifying reality. This God, who had the dreadful power to consign me there for all eternity if I didn't go to Mass on Sundays, or if I ate meat on a Friday, or married a Protestant without permission to do so, could strike me dead at any moment. For now, I wasn't going to Mass on Sundays; I was eating meat on a Friday; I had married a Protestant in a Protestant church, and so I was piling up sins 'in the eyes of The Roman Catholic Church' as fast as I could go. I would *have* to do something about it. I suddenly remembered that I was a child of Mary: I would have to seek her intercession again, for she was the 'refuge of sinners'. I proposed to leave my husband, go back into a convent, get to confession there, and tell the priest I had married a Protestant without permission and hadn't been to Mass for at least a couple of years. I started to pray to St Jude, the patron saint of hopeless cases, and made my plans.

Chapter 7

On The Run

There is a well known expression that 'man proposes
and God disposes'. I had, in the Post Office, a few
pounds of my own money, which I withdrew, and
waited till the weekend, when my husband would be
going fishing many miles away with some of his
angling friends. After he had set off I flung a few
things into a suitcase, and left a note on the
mantlepiece. It said: 'I'm leaving you. Don't ever try
to find me because you won't.' Off I went to
Manchester. I had never been there before but I knew
it had a convent of the same order as I had been in.

I found it eventually and asked to see the Mother
Superior. I told my story, expressed my great desire to
get to confession, and declared my intention to stay in
the convent, this time for good. The Mother Superior
coldly informed me that I was not married in the eyes
of the Church. She wasn't telling me anything I didn't
already know, but she had come to the conclusion that
I was undoubtedly married in the eyes of the law, and
so the bishop would have to be consulted on that point
before she could let me through the enclosure. I would
have to stay in one of the visitors' rooms until she had
seen him.

I spent the next three to four days in a small room,
thinking every time I heard a footstep that someone
was coming for me. This would mean either confession to the convent chaplain, or an interview with the

bishop. The Mother Superior never came back to see me; I never got to confession; and no word came from the bishop.

One afternoon, while I was sitting reading the life of some saint, an inner voice began to say to me: 'Go back to your husband, go back, go back!' The voice got louder and louder, and more and more insistent, until I felt absolutely driven to fling my few belongings back into my case, put on my hat and coat, and go out into the corridor. I didn't meet a soul.

Without anyone seeing me, I passed through several doors including the open front door. There might not seem to be anything unusual about that; but the doors in these convents have no handles on them, and they are opened only by those nuns who carry passkeys on their belts. At the time I never gave it another thought. I went through the grounds and out on to the road, and still the voice was saying to me: 'Go back, go back'.

I reached the station in the city, looked up a train to Glasgow, and sent my husband a telegram, which read: 'Meet me Glasgow Central, such and such a time'. I had exactly enough money left to buy my train ticket back to Glasgow, and not one halfpenny more. I felt a complete and utter fool. My attempts to get back into Holy Mother Church had been a complete fiasco. St Jude hadn't half let me down!

Would my husband be there? Would he take me back again after my running away from him? Would he insist on knowing where I had been? I couldn't tell him because he didn't know I was a Roman Catholic, and if he found out there would very likely be murder committed in Glasgow Central station. If he wasn't there when I arrived I hadn't even my bus fare back to where we lived — (six pence in today's money). As the train neared Glasgow and passed over the Clyde, I said to myself, 'If he's not there to meet me, it's going to be the end for me tonight in that river.' At the time I really meant it: but when the train drew into the Central, there he was, standing on the platform! He was so glad to see me back at the time that he forgot to ask me where I had been! Again I had made an attempt to find the way to peace with God, but had gone the wrong way about it. I was yet to be led by the right way, but that was still in the future.

Chapter 8

A Temporary Respite

We talked things over and decided that we'd try once more to make a go of our marriage. In an attempt to patch things up, and for the sake of my husband's saving face, I started to attend his church. This was merely an outward gesture, which had no meaning as far as I was concerned, for I certainly was not going to unite in worship with heretics and I was not going to handle a Bible, the forbidden book. But before very long I found myself accepted into membership of that church. This was done through my husband's man-oeuvring without my knowledge or consent. Wild as I was at the time I had to put a face on things and avoid a scene, so accepted the situation.

It seemed that I had become a member of a Protestant church. Outwardly I was a nominal Christian, at heart still a convinced Roman Catholic; and yet I still knew nothing whatever of salvation or of the new creation to be found through Jesus Christ. I still had not found the right way — or rather, God had not yet led me to it. Does He not have His appointed time, and surely He will do nothing outside it?

Time marched on and things did not improve for me. Once again our marriage started to come unstuck, and we were back to square one. There was nothing to hold it together. Attending a dead and a powerless form of worship together on a Sunday couldn't improve us. It could not change us, it did not save us, and it could not put right all the things that were wrong. So things went from bad to worse, and from worse to impossible. Eventually our marriage ended where so many marriages end in a situation like this — heading straight for shipwreck.

What was left for me now? I had been a nun once, faithless to her religious vows. Now I was on the very brink of being a wife faithless to her marriage vows. I had sought three times to find the way to peace with God, but I had not found it. Was there then to be no fulfilling of the promise in His word, 'Seek and ye shall find'? In misery and desperation I started to make plans to run away again, and this time it wouldn't be to a convent. I was going to try to get a little pleasure out of life for a change, and seek elsewhere for all the things my marriage had not given me. It was no use making any more abortive attempts to get back into Holy Mother Church or to seek the intercession of Our Lady. She had 'put paid' to that idea when I had tried it.

But there was a snag to my plans for running away this time — lack of money. I had none of my own left so I would have to wait a bit and try to get my hands on my husband's wallet. That was a very difficult proposition. I would need to bide my time; then I would grab it and disappear, this time definitely for good. Our marriage was completely on the rocks. Things had come to the point of no return. My life was intolerable. The immediate outlook was as bleak as could be, and looming in the distant future was the distinct possibility of an eternity in hell.

Chapter 9

Divine Intervention

A miserable existence with a lost eternity to follow: that was how matters stood when God stepped into this hopeless situation. Looking back now I think I can see the reason why. When things had got to that pitch we had qualified for His intervention. What was our qualification? We were both lost, as lost as any two people could be. The religious man was lost and he didn't know it, and the ex-religious woman was lost too, and only too well did she know it. But does not our Lord Himself tell us that that's the very reason He came to this earth? He came to seek and to save the lost. He came not to call the righteous, but sinners to repentance. Does He not tell us that as the Good Shepherd He would leave ninety-nine sheep in the fold and go after just one that was lost?

'For thus saith the Lord God; Behold I, even I, will both search my sheep and seek them out'[1].

And so the hand of God started events moving here without either of us being aware.

The papers began to tell of a certain preacher who was coming to Scotland to conduct a crusade in the Kelvin Hall, Glasgow, at the invitation of a church movement called 'Tell Scotland'. I was vaguely interested. What was this man going to tell Scotland? And what was a crusade in 1955? The only crusades I knew anything about were in the history books and

1. Ezekiel 34 v. 11

had been in the Middle Ages. My interest grew. I shelved my plan to run away just for the time being. That could wait a little bit longer until I had been to the Kelvin Hall first to see what this was all about. Anyway, I hadn't yet got my hands on my husband's wallet!

I was curious to see this man, and in due time I went with a bus party from our church. If you think you know how this story is going to end, you are wrong. For the first time in my life I found myself in a vast evangelical gathering in the Kelvin Hall. I had no idea what was going on. There I saw the words, 'I am the Way, the Truth, and the Life'. I had always been taught that Mary was the Way. There I heard for the first time the words, 'Ye must be born again'. What did that mean? Roman Catholics believe that the new birth is received by christening in the Roman Catholic Church, and even that doesn't guarantee heaven. The nearest you can get to that is hoping you will get there, perhaps after many years of terrible suffering and torment by fire in a place called purgatory. If a Roman Catholic were to say that he was sure he was going to heaven, he would be guilty of the sin of presumption. I am perfectly certain that no Roman Catholic, from the Pope downwards, has ever said so. They wouldn't dare do so, for up to the very last minute of life a Roman Catholic can be guilty of mortal sin not confessed to a priest and so be sent to hell. No absolution from a priest — no salvation.

What I heard in the Kelvin Hall was to me a new way of preaching from the Bible — very different from anything I had ever heard. Still, the Bible was really a forbidden book to me. I am well aware that Roman Catholics are allowed to read it today, but it was absolutely forbidden in my day. This is a privilege only afforded them by Pope John XXIII.

My interest was well and truly aroused. I began to wonder. I went back again to the Kelvin Hall. There was something different here, something I couldn't define. Questions were arising in my mind. Was there salvation outside the Church of Rome? No, there couldn't be. It was a mortal sin even to think such a thing was possible. This preacher, however, said that salvation was obtained through believing in the finished work of Christ at Calvary, not through belonging to any particular church. It was simply repenting and accepting what Christ's work offered. I had been taught that Calvary was unfinished, and renewed daily in every sacrifice of the Mass.

Every Roman Catholic priest in the world is taught that after he is ordained he has the power to bring the Lord Jesus Christ down from heaven to enter bodily into the elements of bread and wine. These must then be elevated, held up for the worship of those present, and offered to God the Father as an unblooded sacrifice for sin. To hear that Calvary was a finished work sounded like blasphemy to me. Was there forgiveness of sin outside of the Roman Catholic confessional? All my training and indoctrination denied such a possibility. But this preacher kept asking us to repent and come to Christ for the forgiveness of sins. Who was right?

I forgot to run away. I forgot all about getting my hands on my husband's wallet. I went back repeatedly to the Kelvin Hall, ten times in all, for I was unwittingly starting for the fourth time, to seek a way to peace with God. But I did not go forward at any of the meetings, for two main reasons: one was fear of my husband, and the other (and I supposed, the far greater fear) was fear of being involved with heretics. In spite of my fears, however, the quest was on once more. Was there the tiniest possible hope that there was a way to peace with God that bypassed the Roman Catholic Church? Could I get rid of my sins through direct dealing with God and not have to tell a priest what I had done? Had I not committed mortal sins all those years by not going to Mass and by attending Protestant worship? Could it possibly be true that the Lord Jesus wasn't really bodily present on Roman Catholic altars? I roamed the streets at times, while my husband was at work, wondering, puzzling, hoping I could find out the answers to these questions. But where? If only I could discover for certain who was right! It now became the most important thing in life for me to try to discover the truth. Nothing else mattered.

Chapter 10

Gloriously Saved

Three months later there was a follow-up campaign to the 'Tell Scotland' Crusade in a town that was within reach by bus. Still seeking the answers to all the questions that were troubling me, I attended the meetings in one of the large churches there.

Do you know the words of Psalm 107? 'There was none to help, hungry and thirsty their soul fainted in them. Then they cried unto the Lord in their trouble, and he saved them out of their distresses'.

Night after night I went into that town to these meetings.

On the Saturday my husband went away for the day to fish on the Clyde and in the evening I went to the campaign meeting. There, that night, as the evangelist preached, I knew for certain that the Lord Jesus had settled the question of sin once and forever by His death, and that at Calvary the work of atonement had been finished. No priest could renew it in the so-called 'sacrifices of the Mass'. In belief and the deepest repentance the burden was lifted and all my guilt was taken away. I had confessed my sins to the Great High Priest alone. At last I had been led into the right way to peace with God.

That, however, is not the end of this story, it's only part of it.

When the evangelist made the appeal that night, I left my place and went to the front of the church, the only one; the first convert of the campaign, born again into the Kingdom of God. The evangelist dealt with me himself. I told him I had been a Roman Catholic all my life, whether practising or lapsed, and that was the only religion I knew anything about.

'Never mind about that,' he said, dismissing the information with a wave of his hand as if it was of no importance!

He made me promise to do two things. One was to start reading the Bible every day, and the other, to tell my husband when I went home what I had done, and that I was saved. Not until I was on the bus on the way home did the implication of these two promises begin to dawn on me; to read the Bible, and to tell him.

Tell him!

Read the Bible, the forbidden book, a book I had never opened in my life, and by now I was forty years of age!

Read the Bible, and tell him!

I didn't know which was worse!

At midnight my husband arrived home from his fishing. His train had been delayed. He was tired, cold and hungry. I met him at the door and told him I was saved. It most certainly was not the right moment. Ladies, don't ever try to tell a man anything of importance when his stomach is empty. If you want a sympathetic hearing, feed him first!

The next day I opened the Bible, the forbidden book, while my husband was at work. I didn't make a very good job of that either; I opened it at a chapter of 'begats' and I couldn't understand a word of it!

Chapter 11

In The Wilderness

Now began for me a wilderness experience for three whole years. All thoughts of running were at an end. My life had been completely changed, and I knew now where my duty lay as a wife, in fulfilling my marriage vows and in facing up to whatever lay ahead.

Here I was left high and dry as a newly-born Christian with no help or encouragement from minister, church or evangelical fellowship. I came into the spiritual world in exactly the same way as I came into the physical one, unwelcome, unwanted and finding no spiritual home.

Psalm 107 says: 'They wandered in the wilderness in a solitary way', and my way was so solitary!

For me there was no spiritual food from the ministry of God's word, no guidance or instruction in the way of the Christian life, no help with the reading of the Bible. There was no one to give me the hand of fellowship. I was left to struggle on as well as I could. It was terribly difficult, at one go, to get rid of all the beliefs and practices I had been taught and come into simple faith in the finished work of Christ. It took time.

Then there was the opposition of my husband to contend with. He thought I had developed religious mania. He had naturally no understanding of what had happened to me. So, for me, following Christ was not going to be a bed of roses. I've since come to the conclusion that if our witness doesn't cost us anything, if we don't have to suffer something, no matter how small, for His name's sake, then, I think, we're not worth our salt as Christians. Our discipleship isn't worth tuppence, and the works of God are not being shown in us.

At the beginning of my story I spoke of the beggar whose eyes the Lord Jesus had opened on the Sabbath day. As soon as that man received his sight he had to bear witness to the fact, and his witness brought him nothing but trouble. Hasn't it been the same to a greater or lesser degree for countless believers ever since? For how many has the miracle of opened eyes not meant trouble?

Day by day I struggled on the best I could. I kept the promise I had made, and I persevered in reading the Bible without any help. Little by little, as I stuck mainly to parts of the New Testament which I could understand, light came.

Psalm 78 says: 'Can God furnish a table in the wilderness'?

I began to haunt the library for religious books, especially religious history. Very soon I discovered that church history, written by non-Catholic historians, was something very different from what I had learned at school. Through time, slowly but surely, bit by bit, I studied and read myself out of all belief in the claims of the Roman Catholic Church. But it hadn't been an easy task. Lifetime fears are very difficult things to shake off.

So, alone and sometimes very discouraged, with no-one to advise me, I read and searched and studied. Sometimes the terrible fear came upon me that perhaps I had taken the wrong step after all. At long last, however, I did come out of firm belief in the infallibility of the Pope into the sure and certain knowledge of the infalliblity of God's Word, 'which alone is able to make us wise unto salvation through faith which is in Christ Jesus'[1]. Sometimes I got so interested in what I was reading that there were burnt offerings for my husband's dinner when he came home from work! And like the Lord he did not always find them acceptable! When he discovered that I was reading religious books and letting the dinner burn he considered me ready for Larbert asylum. Starved of the real preaching of the Word, and never coming into contact with other Christians, I still hung on desperately to the knowledge of the truth that had made me free.

The Bible says: 'In all thy ways acknowledge him and he shall direct thy paths'[2].

1. *2nd Timothy 3 v. 15*
2. *Proverbs 3 v. 6*

Chapter 12

The Fellowship Of Believers

Through reading the Word of God for myself, there came the time when I desired to undergo believers' baptism, by immersion, only I didn't know how to go about it. I knew absolutely nothing of the denominational differences in churches. I had never been inside any other church, except the one of which my husband was an elder: but I had a great desire and determination to go through the baptismal waters.

Seeing the name, 'Baptist Church', advertised in the local paper as being in a town not very far away, and thinking I might get what I was looking for, I sneaked off one Sunday to the evening service when my husband had to go to work. Once inside I knew that it was the right place for me. The sermon that night was nothing to do with baptism but it was the preaching of the Word, the first ministry I had heard since the night I was converted three years previously. It was something for which I was starving, and the hand of fellowship was offered to me at the door of that church for the first time in my life. I determined that this was the church to which I would go in future.

Alas, when my husband found out where I had been to he had other ideas, and they did not include my going amongst 'Hallelujahs', as he called them. He wasn't going to have it. On the Sundays that he had to go to work, I was to attend the church where he was an elder. But for once he had met his match. For the first

time in my married life I suddenly remembered I had a
mind of my own, and that mind, to my husband's
astonishment, was going to be asserted.

Nothing would induce me to go back to a dead form
of worship and nothing was going to stop me attending
the church which I felt God had led me to. On this one
point I was determined I would not give in, and I
didn't.

So there was an angry kirk elder and a divided
house. The sword of division was between us now and
it became even sharper. That, though, is what the
Lord promised His disciples. He came not to bring
peace but division in households and the only peace
He promised us is peace with God.

Eventually I saw the minister of the church I was
attending and I asked to be baptised. I had not seen a
baptismal service and I had not the slightest idea of
what to expect. The minister agreed to my request. I
would have to tell my husband, of course, and he
would be invited to the service. Tell my husband! I
had had every intention of being baptised without his
knowing anything about it.

'Tell him! Oh no,' I said. 'You baptise me first and
I'll tell him afterwards.'

The minister just looked at me. I think he saw that I
hadn't the slightest intention of telling my husband
and I'm perfectly certain he must have been thinking
to himself, 'I've got a right one here!'

'Baptism is a public witness of your faith in Christ,'
he said to me. 'It's not something you can do in secret.
Your husband must be told you've asked for baptism
and he must be invited to the service.'

My legs turned to jelly. The only thing I could think

of saying was, 'You tell him.'

'Certainly,' he said, 'I'll come and see him.'

Home I went to tell my husband that a Baptist minister was coming to see him. I will not repeat here what he said! I had another worry now. What if he flung the poor man into the canal? The minister duly arrived, and to my great surprise my husband did not fling him into the canal. Instead he sat and listened very meekly as, for the first time in his life, he was challenged about salvation; challenged about the difference in being a member of a church and being a member of the body of Christ by the new birth. The minister invited him to come and see me baptised, and to my horror he said he would! That was the one thing I did not want. I did not want him to come anywhere near the church. I was afraid of being humiliated. I was opposing his wishes by consorting with 'Hallelujahs' and I dreaded the possibility of what he might say or do in the church if he came. So I prayed hard that he would not come. It was of course a selfish prayer. Selfish to the core. God answered it, though.

It wasn't long before the effect of the minister's visit wore off and my husband once again began to voice his displeasure at the step I had taken. In a fit of anger at my refusal to go with him to his church any more on a Sunday, he flung up his eldership, resigned from membership, giving no reason, and vowed he would never set foot in a church again. That was that! Then he wouldn't be coming to see me baptised: I could relax.

One thing was certain — he would never, never be converted. I was absolutely convinced of that. I prayed vaguely for it to happen, of course, just out of a sense of duty as his wife, but it was the unbelieving

prayer of an unbelieving wife. After all, he couldn't
see his need. Besides, hadn't he been an elder for
twenty-three years? Hadn't he been one of the pillars
of his church? Wasn't he looked upon by everybody as
a model of respectability, who didn't do the things that
other men did? He just couldn't understand why his
church was no longer good enough for me. He had no
time for my religious nonsense. It only angered and
upset him.

Chapter 13

The God Who Saves

The night for my baptism arrived. In spite of his vow, my husband had changed his mind many times about whether he would come to the church or not, and so I hoped against hope that he would not. All my prayers were useless. They might as well have been addressed to the empty air, for he came, and in the mood he was in there was the distinct possibility that he would make a scene. Why had the minister insisted on inviting him?

With a sinking feeling I set off with him to the church. My hopes had dropped to zero. In my disappointment I remember praying that I would just die when I came out of the water and go to be with the Lord. I was so fed up that I felt that would be the easiest solution to all my troubles. I just didn't want to face any more of them.

The first half of the service was conducted and the sermon preached. Baptism wasn't mentioned, but rather the focus was on salvation. It was a challenge to the unsaved present to repent, to believe, and to accept Christ as Saviour. Then I went forward to enter the baptismal waters. In the plan and purposes of God for each of our lives, His timing is always perfect.

The congregation started up the hymn, 'O Jesus, I have promised to serve Thee to the end'. Then it happened. Like a lightning flash the power of God fell and it struck my husband right where he was sitting. It transfixed him. He became for the moment absolutely paralysed, unable to move hand or foot and unable to sing another note of the hymn. In what he could only afterwards describe as an experience of brilliant inner light, he heard the voice of God. These are the words that were spoken to him: 'You must either accept or reject. This will be your only chance'. In one split second he saw, his eyes were opened, and he knew himself to be a sinner in need of salvation. As I went under the water, symbolically into death with Christ, he repented, he believed, and he was saved. That night, at the very moment when I passed through the waters of baptism, by the miraculous intervention of God, John passed from death to life. He had entered that church dead in trespasses and sins, he left it alive for evermore!

Knowing nothing of what happened, I trailed off to the ladies' room hoping to go to Glory, full of the joy of rising to newness of life, and longing to meet the Lord. Instead of departing to be with Christ, I had to go home on the bus with John. He was white and silent, and I wondered what was brewing. Like a typical Scot he took his time before he told me what had happened. When he did, may the Lord forgive me, I didn't believe it! I couldn't believe it!

But it was true: it had happened. The following Sunday morning we were sitting together in that church, one in Christ Jesus.

Four weeks later he followed me through the waters of baptism. God had indeed answered my prayers that John would not come to the church that night. His answer had been 'No'. Why? Because He had some better thing in store; far, far better than I had ever dreamed of. God answers prayers but not always as we might wish. He does not guarantee it will be 'Yes'. When He says 'No', it is because He loves us and sees the things we ask for could never give blessing.

God saved both of us individually in His own appointed time. He saved our marriage. He reconciled us to Himself and He reconciled us to each other.

Ours became a union truly made by God: the marriage, once on the rocks, became firmly established upon the Rock. To me the Lord fulfilled the promise in His Word, 'Seek and ye shall find'; to John He said, 'Choose'.

So 'he led us forth by the right way, that we might go to a city of habitation'[1].

[1] *Psalm 107 v.7*

Chapter 14

Peace At Last

Soon after my husband was converted he lost his job and he never worked again. A few months later it was discovered that he had a fatal disease. In the month of February 1971, John passed into the presence of his Lord. He has gone on ahead to the city of habitation. The marriage tie was severed but he is in Glory, wonderfully saved by that split-second opportunity. Where would he be today if he had not taken it? God not only opened his eyes to salvation, but also to the deadness of a formal worship without life or power. He opened mine, not only to the new birth, but to all the futility and superstition of my previous efforts to find God's peace.

Psalm 107 says: 'He brought them out of darkness and the shadow of death and brake their bands in sunder'.

God brought me out of prison conditions from behind locked convent doors.

He also brought me out of fear and bondage into glorious freedom and the knowledge of how to 'worship him in spirit and in truth'[1].

With the beggar in John's gospel I also can say: 'One thing I know, that whereas I was blind, now I see'[2].

[1] *John 4 v24*
[2] *John 9 v 25*

I found God indeed to be the God of the hopeless situation.

Is there anyone, I wonder, who has read this story and who feels that his personal circumstances couldn't be worse. I wonder if somebody has read it who has to struggle on in a divided house, and things seem just hopeless.

Maybe somebody has read this who thinks that everything necessary has been done to get to heaven by joining a church, and being on a membership roll. To you especially I would say, remember that my husband was an elder for twenty-three years. All his adult life, to the age of nearly sixty-one, he was a member of a church, and he was not saved. I did not tell him that: God told him. I leave his conversion to speak for itself.

To each and everyone of you who reads this story I would say, no matter how difficult your circumstances or how great your need, no matter what your problems are, you can discover even as I did that God is the God who is abundantly able to deal with the situation, however hopeless it seems. He is the God who is able to bring you through your circumstances, whatever they are, into the glorious and satisfying life of peace which the world cannot give — peace with God.

1. O Give thanks unto the Lord, for he is good:
for his mercy endureth for ever.

2. Let the redeemed of the Lord say so,
whom he hath redeemed from the hand of the enemy;

3. And gathered them out of the lands, from the east, and from the west,
from the north and from the south.

4. They wandered in the wilderness in a solitary way;
they found no city to dwell in.

5. Hungry and thirsty,
their soul fainted in them.

6. Then they cried unto the Lord in their trouble,
and he delivered them out of their distresses.

7. And he led them forth by the right way,
that they might go to a city of habitation.

8. Oh that men would praise the Lord for his goodness.
and for his wonderful works to the children of men!

9. For he satisfieth the longing soul,
and filleth the hungry soul with goodness.

10. Such as sit in darkness and in the shadow of death,
being bound in affliction and iron;

11. Because they rebelled against the words of God,
and contemned the counsel of the most High:

12. Therefore he brought down their heart with labour;
they fell down, and there was none to help.

13. Then they cried unto the Lord in their trouble,
and he saved them out of their distresses.

14. He brought them out of darkness and the shadow of death,
and brake their bands in sunder.

15. Oh that men would praise the Lord for his goodness,
and for his wonderful works to the children of men!

16. For he hath broken the gates of brass,
and cut the bars of iron in sunder.

Psalm 107 v 1 - 16.

EPILOGUE

How was it that Alicia, baptised as a child, raised in a convent, taking vows as a nun, attending Mass, was still far away from God? Was she not in the right Church doing the right things? What more could she have done to find God's favour? Was she always in His good books without realising it?

These questions may well have arisen while you have read this story and, of course, they focus on the very heart of the issue. To Alicia as she grew up, as for very many, the Church was the source of salvation. As she belonged to the Church and went through the ritual, prayed, attended services and occasionally fasted, she believed all would be well. All was not well, however, because God was still very distant and promises she read seemed hollow. The lesson she had to learn was that salvation is not found in a Church but in a Person. While we rely on our religious acts and sacraments we fail to place our trust in Christ alone.

Jesus once described a religious man who entered the temple. He was glad he was not like other men, his religion making a difference. He was outwardly upright and had every reason to consider that God would take notice of him. As a result he came to One whom he felt sure would receive him because of who he was and what he had done. Next to him was a notorious sinner, a publican. This man did not raise his head heavenwards but rather struck his breast and cried out for God to be merciful to him, a sinner. Jesus records that the latter left, right with God.

What was the basic difference between the two? The religious man, in common with many who frequent churches in our day, saw himself as a sinner, yet as a heaven-deserving sinner. He had 'done his best' and felt sure that God would take notice. He 'was not as bad as others' and thanked God for this fact. The publican, though, had no illusions about his state. His mind was not focused on justice but mercy. He knew only too well that sin deserved punishment and his sin was hell-deserving. In this lay the difference between these two men, and the difference between being set right with God and being turned away.

For Alicia, God had to bring her to a place where she no longer looked to do something for God but rather looked to Him alone to do something for her. What could God do? The message she believed is the message of the Bible, which records that God has done all that is necessary. If prayers, church attendance, charity and the like can set us right with God, why did Jesus come and why did He die? The Scriptures declare that He came to bear a burden we could bear no longer, our sin. By dying on the cross He took the place of those who trust Him. He was not worthy of death; we are. He had earned God's favour and approval; we haven't. The Bible proclaims no self-improvement plan but rather a substitution: Christ dying in my place that I may be set right with God, no longer under His condemnation. On the basis of His life and death, the risen Lord Jesus Christ invites death-meriting, hell-deserving sinners to come to Him and be set right. To do so involves turning our back on sin and the past life and taking Him at His word.

What are we to believe? Simply that, for those who place their complete trust in Him, their sin is placed to His charge. As by His death He settled the account once and for all, we may know for a certainty that God will forgive all who place their trust in Him. Salvation is a matter of trust in Christ who alone could do the work of paying our debt and winning God's approval.

But surely, you may say, we must also live a good life. Yes indeed, the Christian does live in obedience to God, not in order to win His favour but rather as a result of God's transforming power. When a man or woman is set right with God, the Holy Spirit is given to that person to live within them. It is God's Spirit who is then at work in them changing their desires and leading them in God's way.

For many religious people there is continuing uncertainty about whether they will ever attain the necessary standard required for God's approval. The more they strive, the more conscious they become of God's holy standard. The true Christian, however, has a peace which passes understanding. For them Christ is their complete confidence. Not only has He done what no one else could do, but God has told in the Bible of His acceptance of Jesus' work. They know that God invites them to trust in Christ and having done so He assures them of their acceptance by granting them His peace.

If you lack this calm assurance and resultant peace in believing, then take up a Bible and begin to read in the New Testament in John's Gospel. Ask God to open your eyes to who Jesus is and to what He has done. His promise is that those who seek Him shall find Him and the door will be opened to those who knock.

May Alicia's story be the means of you also seeking and finding her Saviour.

P.R.